MW01242772

It's Dark on This Side of Heaven

—

Nora Yolanda

About the Book

—

It's Dark on This Side of Heaven is a collection of short stories and poetry that will give you insight into the mind of Nora Yolanda. The book will take you on a journey through pain, confusion, revelation, and love. Which is all centered around Nora's experience of growing up and living in the inner city of Baltimore.

The title reference to heaven is symbolic of the different parts of Baltimore City. The darkness described represents the mental conditioning and slavery of many who live there. It also represents some of the battles that Nora herself have dealt with mentally that in the past kept her from thriving in her life. This read was designed to challenge you mentally and is packed with gems from cover to cover.

"This book was a way for me to heal and purge myself of the world and all its issues. To discover what honored my soul, and it wasn't hate, confusion, black versus white or following any one religion. But honoring my soul had more to do with loving myself and how to allow peace to be upon me despite the conditions around me." — Nora

CONTENTS

OH GIVE THANKS

———

Give thanks for everything that occurs even when eyes cannot see the beauty in it, yet the heart and soul knows that it is well and that it is a gift. Giving thanks is a gift that you choose to receive freely from the universe and it opens up every door that one can imagine. So here I am saying thank you for the desire to be grateful. Thank you for that which is perceived to be and thank you for that which is.

I press on,
I keep going,
out of my soul,
I press on

THE PRESS ON

Out of my soul I press on
In my spirit I keep going
Taking a moment to gain strength – I press on
I press on, I keep going, I press on
I press on, and I keep going
I press on, I keep going, out of my soul, I press on
My strength is renewed
I keep going – The press on.

How are you pressing forward?

Love is as beautiful as the morning's glow

LOVE

Love is a truth that the world
shall know; love is the guide that
will light the way, love of self,
love of life, love for all is a love
divine. *Love is as beautiful as the
morning's glow; it's as pure as the
quieting mind and peaceful as the night
when the moon is sure of itself — love.*

I escaped bondage,
A place in my mind

PEACE,
IT CAME FROM THE HEAVENS

The battlefield is outside
It's like a war zone outside
Man it's like a jungle outside
The Vietnam War is outside
And the helicoptor sounds
Don't mean that you're being
swept off of the ground
Taken to safety? No.
They've come to shoot you down
I get up, I get down, I get up – and I
stay up
Because although there is a war going
on outside
I've got victory screaming on the
inside of me
Because yes I come from these
same streets
But I made it out
Out of the conditioning
The conditioning that paralyzes thee
And says hate the skin your in
I made it out of the thoughts that had
me believe
That I was trapped
Trapped in a city so cold
Where all you're ever told is what you
won't be
I made it out because one-day peace
found me and it came,
Peace, It came from the heavens
It was as quiet as the wind can be
And it found me in a time when life
seemed most chaotic

It found me in a time when thoughts
traveled my brain like a train going to
a place called infinity
It found me in a time when my heart
was as heavy as a trillion
weights and my energy had been
depleted to zero
It found me when the world was still spinning
but seemed to be spinning out of control as
if God himself had taken his hands off of
the wheel
And after I had fallen upon my knees
for what seemed to be the
millionth time
Peace came – And it came from
the heavens
I had called on it before
but it didn't show up then
But then it came just in time
I escaped bondage, A place in my mind
Reprogrammed right in the middle of
the battlefield
Peace saved me
And it came from the heavens.

How can you fine peace where there is chaos and confusion?

I won't die tonight;
God is on my side

He is the voice of all people – God

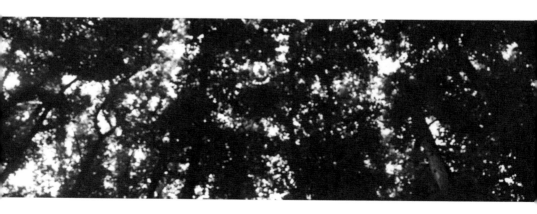

FAR FROM AN ATHEIST

Who is God to me
Undefined mystery
Maker of the birds the trees and the unseen
Keeper of all things
Who is God to me?
Protector over troubles unknown to me
He sits in a place in my heart
He is the voice of all people – God
He allows us the freedom to somewhat comprehend
his beauty, splendor, his majesty
As I look up at the clouds
The blues, the whites, the combinations of color
Color? What is this I see?
Given names by man but identity from God
Who is God to me?
Protector over all things
Trying to understand who he is
is not fair to who he is
A man cannot comprehend all things
How do you understand who God is?
How do you begin?
We label him Allah, Jehovah, Jesus
We give him many names but he is all things seen
and unseen
Every word is God. Hope and faith are God.
Death, sadness, tears and triumphs are God
Adversity and over comers are God
Stars that sparkle in the night
A baby's cry, mother's love
He is the voice of your first and last love
He is assurance to the hooker who sells her body
"I won't die tonight; God is on my side"

He is comfort to the mother who works overtime.
He is the trust that her children will see the payoff
He is the smile on the face of death
He is the laughter from our ancestors who came out of
slavery while being whipped
He is the hope that our sons have behind bars
He is pollen to the bees
Water to the trees
He is the earth beneath my feet
He is faith the size of a mustard seed
Who is God to me? Who is God to me?
Who is he?
He is a feeling,
hairs on my arms that rise at the mention of
his name
He is the feeling and the reason for the feeling
He is the order of the planets
the arrangement of the night and day
He is the maker of every human being
The sweat that falls from my hair
the brow that protects my eyes
He is it and a creator of it
He used one breath to create all things
Can you really understand what that means?
One breath and there it is all that you see.
He is a chance to know him
He is the idea before the idea that there must be
something greater out there
But then he is the revelation that he is not out
but within
Who is God to me?
Keeper of all things.

Who is God to you?

Does your soul speak to you? Do you even know its voice?

THIS IS ALL YOU NEED TO KNOW

Does your soul speak to you in truth?
Does it tell you that you're here for a purpose?
Can you even hear what it is saying to you?
Or does the external dialogue scream louder than
the soft voice of your soul going against all that
which is truth?
Do you know where you are going or thought you
knew where you were going until the voice you
heard spoke louder than the voice within?
Is it truth that you seek or do false truths find you
when you're sitting alone in your sacred place and
you realize the world has found you?
Does your soul speak to you and tell you that you're
here for a purpose?
Or do earthly reviews tell you that you are
worthless?
Does your soul guide you and you shy away from
these things?
These things they exist on the outside of you
Yet your soul is speaking, telling you what it re-
quires of you
Does your soul speak to you?
Do you even know its voice?
This is all you need to know.

What is your soul saying to you?

There's a sweet, sweet sound that travels through me but it's quiet.

SOUND OF GOD

There's a sweet, sweet sound that travels through me yet it's quiet. I think it's the voice of God because it's so gentle and kind. It has to be God whispering; it has to be him whispering love through the inside of me. Every part of me is filled with light that I couldn't have received from any place but him. I cannot hear this voice with my ears but I know it's a sound from the way it feels. It's a subtle base that I feel and I light up because of it. How lovely a sound that I feel - such a beautiful way to live with the voice of God traveling through me.

HARLEM NY 2015

Here in N.Y after the Freddy Gray murder with the rev club – a group of revolutionaries that found me at what the world now calls ground zero but to me it's just a few blocks away from my home. A place I try not to visit much because of the soul murder that occurs on the streets every day. North Avenue (Penn North) is filled with people feigning to escape the conditions that they live in – trying to escape, but with no clue how to, so they use crack, heroin, and now some new age drugs and pills "got dem mollies out." I hear the dope boys in my head as I see the faces of those trying to get away from it all - the feign on the corner begins to elevate to a place that's beyond the corner where he stands slumped over but going up, up, up and away. Leaving a place of lost hopes and dreams born differed.

I met the group while at the library, there to use the internet – I was looking for a job, checking my emails and searching for the courage that I had lost somewhere along the way to dream – day after day looking in the eyes of lifeless beings those faces those lost dreams began to strip me of my hope-fulness, I had cared for them so much, but I had to put my blinders on so that I could dream for me again – there was no room left to dream for them anymore.

As I left the library I met this kid, little Bobby is what the guys from the group called him, he was about 13 with so much innocence accompanied with passion about the revolution and hope for our people. He had virgin hope, it was untouched, untainted and the guys egged him on "that's little Bobby right there." He gonna tell everybody about the revolution." And I worried a bit, I worried that his hopes were too high, that he believed that things would change sooner than they would, I worried that after the smoke and cameras disappeared and the chants and marches were over that the hopeless souls would stare him in his face and remind him that things were the same for his people.

I guess I thought he would become like me in that moment – once a warrior and fighter for what's right but had been knocked down so many times that the overflowing hope became but a little flicker on the inside of me but it was still there because here I was listening to this group tell me about their leader and how he had a plan to free the people and make the world a better place. "Hey", he said, "you wanna join the revolutionary club?" I guess that little bit of hope was all I needed.

5:45 am

I quietly crept out of the room where I was sleep-ing because the girls were still resting (two really

beautiful souls passionate about women's rights and downright pure feminist who also cared about the treatment of young black men by the police) as I came out of the room, there Taye was on the couch where he had spent the night – the apartment in Brooklyn was crowded with revolutionaries of all ages and races. Taye was a revolutionary from the ATL; he was up this morning teaching himself how to speak Spanish. Taye is always intensely studying, he's either reading - Bob Avakian the basics or the revolutionary paper, something aiding in the progression of the revolution and he's always using words and phrases that I'm to proud to ask the meaning, so I pretend to know and then I do my research later. Discussing things like communism and communist parties, Emancipation you know the stuff most revolutionaries discuss. It's hard not to want to learn more around him, he inspires me to dig a little deeper for knowledge and be a bit more conscious.

It had gotten so bad that I couldn't even look
them in their eyes
I knew so much that they didn't - knowing that they
are trapped in a trap and wanting to set them free
but couldn't
It had gotten so bad that I wouldn't dare give them
contrary information against what has shaped them
This knowledge that has put them into a hold where
it chokes them, this knowledge
That they wouldn't have a clue what to do with
That I couldn't even muster up the courage to give
them but courage I wasn't lacking – they say knowl-
edge is power but where did you get it from?
Better yet, when did you get it? How much did you
get? And can you handle that which is given?
It had gotten to the point where I couldn't even
look them in their eyes. But what would it change?
How did it change me?
Did it make me proud to be black?
No, I've always been proud to be me
with a deep connection to these inner city streets.
Did I sympathize for my people?
More so Empathize for my people
Never sympathy, just empathy
because the same pain they feel - I've felt
Looking around at a war zone
Friends in combat with me nursing the wounds
and sometimes having to join in the fight
Oh, I know what it's like to not be conscious
but very conscious of the conditions in which I
grew up in
It had gotten so bad that I couldn't even look them
in their eyes.
It was as if I was holding on to a secret that I had
no right to keep
and the knowledge kept pulling at me, begging me
to set it free
It had gotten so bad that I couldn't even convince
her to smile
Hey, I wasn't smiling
Because somewhere between then and there I had
let him back in

Between to be conscious that he was no good
for me
and I was no good for him although I desperately
wanted to be
To be conscious that I needed to experience the
world a little more
not to be caged in
but to be conscious that I was already free with him
And the limiting mindsets that had been engraved
in us was trying to separate us at best
To be or not to be aware that the universe
destined us to be
until destiny meets now I must wait
Conscious of what it means to live my truth
keep going despite the conditions and conditioning
He's still on my mind from time to time – I digress
It was somewhere between me giving up on all the
things I had tried to convince them not to do
I couldn't convince her to smile, I wasn't smiling
It had gotten so that I couldn't even look her in
the eyes
Because I didn't recognize she - She being me
But I had to look anyway, you see my curiosity was
peeking at me – curious to see what was
happening to her
Who was that in the mirror so overwhelmingly
conscious of what?
The world's views and all of their insecurities accu-
mulated over hundreds of years
When grandma didn't raise me like that
mamma always told me to fight back
Stand tall, head high towards the sky
Church says that's where my help is at
Wisdom shows that's where my strength is at
Momma's voice in the back of my mind
yelling "if they bigger than you, pick up a bat."
But she didn't teach me how to fight this fight
This combat between consciousness of this
and that
women's rights, animal's rights
black lives matter? -But who exactly are we trying to
convince here?

What about these numbers Baltimore?
October with 27 murders in 28 days
helicopter sounds, police patrolling the grounds
And those who need to be reminded haven't looked in the
mirror in a while
To see that, that man he just killed on the street
look just like him
Who are we reminding? Because we've seem to
have forgotten
Every time hoe escapes your mouth to demean her
Your sister, your mother, oh yeah she look just
like her
Who are we reminding?
Every time you criticize that young girl or guy for
being ignorant
but you never took the time to teach them
Remind the police that our lives matter
Remind the people that look like the people that
all lives matter
In the context of love, what's on the agenda?
Animal's rights, their lives matter – are we more
important than them?
When we're all connected – who do we petition
for first?
It had gotten so bad that I couldn't convince him
to fly
because *somewhere along the way of me living*
my dreams
I had clipped my wing
Or maybe the winds had increased
but I was surely flying differently.
Conscious to be or not to be?

Remind the people that look like the people that all lives matter.

We've run this
race before
We've won this
race before

We Act — We don't react
We get strategic and change things
We create our own lanes
And thrive in our communities
We elevate and increase our wealth
Invest it so that we see it again
We celebrate our unique ways
we don't participate in the lies that tell
us that we're demonized
Because we are kings and we are queens
We rise above all things
No matter the situation or our education
Our birthright is to stand tall at all times
At all costs
Keep going through all obstacles
We've run this race before
We've won this race before
We get strong on our run because the
time will come
Where we rise up and rise above it all
The time is here — The time is now
We Act — We don't react.

How are you making a stand right where you are?

BE FREE

Fly young girl fly
It's ok, you don't have to explain why
Why you'd rather go the other way
When everyone else is telling you to go right
Is that right? - No left
But you weren't even thinking direction
You were thinking more like dimensions
Other worlds and universes are calling your name
And they thought they knew you
They thought that they could see you
But they don't have eyes that could see your spirit rise
And they thought you shined bright
When they got a glimpse of what they believe is your light
But in secrete place is dwelling
And you're quiet because your mind perceives magic all of
the time
And just because they can't see your wings, doesn't mean you can't fly
They're still thinking left and right
They perceive you with their eyes
But you're dreaming – manifesting dreams and wings to fly
They thought it was a place on the map
And yes, yes the stars have aligned
So fly young girl fly

Other worlds and universes are calling your name

What is calling you right now?

VIRTUE

———

"Keep hold of your virtue, that which is kind, loving,
peaceful, innocent and pure for it is divine and allow the
gleam in your eye to shine bright"

LOVE CONTINUED

Love has me so encouraged it's like a candle that's always
lit and providing light in what can never be a dark place,
it has me faithful to me and denying all things that don't
comply with what it effortlessly says is the way to be. Love
has me so encouraged to hold on to it a little while longer.
It asks me, "has it ever truly forsaken me?" and I reply
maybe?" and it asks me to take another look, look a little
deeper and then it asks me again – and in my mind I recall
every dark time and there was love right there in a corner
of my mind flickering creating the sparkle in my eye,
waking me up in up in the night just to say thank you for
the light (the hope) I reach it in the morning time.

How does love show up in your life?

It's Dark in this part of heaven

The Gods are dying

CONVERSATION BALTIMORE 2015
from a conversation I overheard

"Yo, I gotta get that kids brains off my shoes, he shot that man and that shit all over my shoes."

Those words, those words – brains off my shoes, kid and man - Same time someone's child. Mind not fully developed to a consciousness that his life deserved more than to have his brains splattered on the streets of Baltimore, now referred to as shit on shoes.

I shake myself as if to shake these words off of me, the weight of it much too heavy to carry – I've got to put them down. *How else can a sweet, kind, gentle, loving spirit exist in a jungle? It's a war zone outside, the Vietnam War is outside and I'm by his side telling him not to die someone loves you although the bullet hole with his precious blood oozing out says otherwise.* Blood stained pavement – He paved them with his blood.

Blood stained pavement
His precious blood paved them

BLOOD STAINED PAVEMENT

Blood stained pavements
His precious blood paved them
Not what was intended for his life?
His energy now roaming the city streets
Seeping into the cracks of the pavement
Living amongst the weeds
No longer able to grow
No longer able to be – be the the savage, the thug
they told him to be.
His lifeless body, blood oozing, energy roaming
the streets
Uneasy rest as he has learned that his rest came too soon
He could've lived another way had he known then what he
discovered on the other side - Blood Stained Pavements.

Write a prayer or an affirmation of love for the inner city.

—

NEW FAMILY
ARKET
CIGARETTES · SODA · NACKS
MILK · ICE CREAM · BILL PAY · EBT
HOLY TEMPLE

Knowledge is power but where did you get it from?
Who gave you that idea?
Does it keep you trapped in the trap that was set to
keep you down?
Do you live in the trenches of your knowledge?
who gave you that idea?
Because if it keeps you bond -Hands tied
Tired, feeling like you can't survive
Feeling as if your kids will die
And its fear that comes alive
It's a lie – who gave you that knowledge?
Who told you those lies?
Ask yourself, why am I not rising to what I know is
inside of me?
I wrestle with a beast
The beast that gave me false information and told me that
knowledge was power
But neglected to tell me that the knowledge that was
given, gave them power over me – that beast

What educational chains are you breaking?

—

(Written in 2007)

This is to pay homage to the 18-year-old young girl who had just went away to college running from a city where she experienced much pain and loss – not really knowing what she was running for. Hoping that one day her dream of being a light to those lost would lead the way out of the darkness. She had no idea how she would do it but she always believed. This is acknowledgment to her and all the other bright chosen spirits that wish to allow their light to shine on the faces of those whose hope is hidden beneath the darkness.

"Let that tiny bit of hope be the foundation you stand on. Soon you'll become that hope"

RUNNING

Running for my home
The crack heads, abandoned kids
And homeless people with no homes and no beds
And everything that's been wrong for so long
Running for the poverty in my streets
The babies having babies
And all the nights of no sleep
The gunshots, sirens
And losing a friend every week
Running for the dope dealers and the dope feigns
'selling their bodies for another hit
I've been running for a murder rate that rises
every year
Running from a fear that death is near
I'm running for all the children whose parents
have died
Some not in the physical but might as well be if
they're not in their lives physically
Running for the safety that doesn't exist in
the home
Because anyone is welcomed in the home to roam
at any time
I've been running, running to get stronger to
bring a new day for my sisters and brothers who
don't know any other way.

"Let that tiny bit of hope be the
foundation you stand on.
Soon you'll become that hope"

Who are you running for?
(besides yourself and why?)

HOME

Baltimore – you still appear beautiful to me, although beauty seen with eyes closed, I open them to see and it is then that I'm reminded that I still have work to do.

You make all of
that ok
Heroin, my friend,
my love, my God

HEROIN — MY GOD

Slumped over, traveling a high a billion
miles beyond the sky
Got right outside of heaven's doorway but he
wouldn't let me in
Fed the devil's side one too many times
Needle to arm, needle to wrist
Tap, tap, tap
A vein nonexistent
Needle to neck as a serpent feigns to
its prey
Pierced skin, it is my demise
My soul has died and it feels so good
No place to stay – that's ok
Kids taken away – ok
You make all of that ok
Heroin, my friend, my love, my God.

BALTIMORE UPRISING /
PEACEFUL PROTEST

Today I was out during the peaceful protest for Freddy Grey and I had the chance to go to the neighborhood where he lived with the rev club. The people were having a celebration to honor his life. It was clear that we all needed a little bit of hope after this week's experience of protests, riots, and news cameras invading our city and treating the people as if they were animals in a zoo that they were just happy to report. The neighborhood was filled, parents were outside with their children enjoying the local performers' rendition of Michael Jackson songs – gonna make a change comes on and although none of the hoopla suggests a change is anywhere in sight the spirits of the people celebrate that only if for a moment change has come.

It stung a bit when
I fell to the ground
but I'm back up

UNEXPECTEDLY

You may have given up on me
But don't count me or better yet count me out
The surprise you'll see when I get up before the count
is out still swinging
Still fighting, still screaming, still throwing punches
Heart beating a little faster, but I'm up
It stung a bit when I fell to the ground but I'm back up
My confidence a little shaky down there
But I got up a, don't count me out
Better yet, count me out
I'd like to see the expression on your face when I get up
swinging and that hit you receive came unexpectedly.

I apologize to all
of the kids who die
before their time,
before their prime.

This is a piece from a letter that I wrote during the time of Trayvon Martin, never really expecting it to be relevant years later. In the letter I apologize to all of the kids who die before their time, before their prime. Now in 2016 there are so many names to pay respect to - then I felt powerless with only my pen and my compassion for their lives but today is different today I am hopeful.

To the little me(s) of the world:
The kids who look like me, talk like me and walk like me but will never get a chance to follow their dreams like me; the ones that'll never know that they are great, beautiful, smart, princes and princess – future kings and queens.

From: your father, mother sister and brother
We tell you to go to school but on the way there you're murdered. We tell you to avoid violence and run but when you run, you're chased and shot dead. Sorry, that the advice we give may cost you your life.

Sorry Black Kids

It's a war zone outside

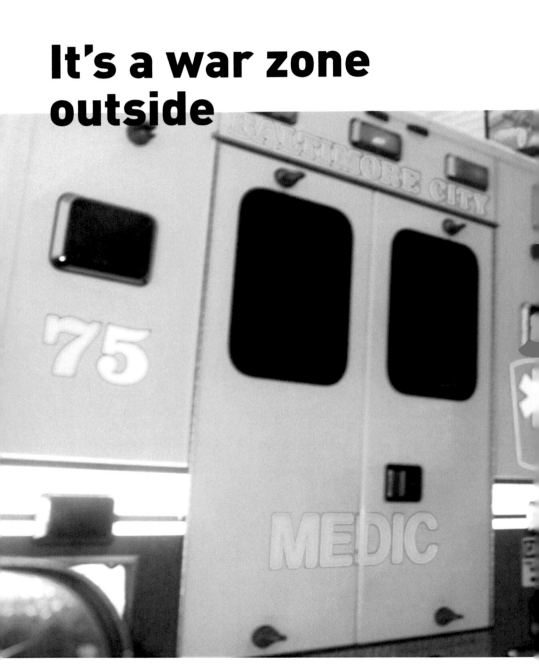

Listening to sirens all through the night and waking up to them with the morning's light – something like that has to affect the mental.

- It's a war zone outside -

Especially when you hear on the radio that there have been 29 murders in 27 days October. I guess I've been trying to detach from it all but what happens when you love – when you love the city that you were raised in? You love the people but not the conditions.

You pray. You work. You love.

His body appears lifeless, no movement, eyes open and blood oozing from his head

---

YOUNG BLACK BODIES, LIFELESS IN THE CITY STREETS

I heard the gunshots outside my window. It was a Sunday night, we were fresh from the morning's service at church and everyone was working in my room tonight. Two sisters both students one at Hopkins working on her master's degree, the other at University of Baltimore studying law and me working on my plan to change the city to put some love into the place where I was raised. But this night my life changed and he changed it.

I heard the gunshots and thought nothing of it; just a typical sound in Baltimore City but an inner prompting told me to go to the window to close the blinds. Before I closed them I peeked out to see – and there he was all alone waiting for me. Underneath the street light and I scream not because I was afraid but call the police I can't do anything with my hands I can barely see what's happening. Everything is a blur and then something switches in me - I've got to go outside he needs me, by then my sister is holding me; you can't go out, "what if the shooter sees you?" I don't care, the block begins to light up and she clears me to go outside or I escape – the people are coming from their houses and next thing I know I'm by his side praying.

Hold on someone loves you, I love you – I'm here hold on and then my soul's language begins to communicate directly with God. Hasham alla se di ough grattas masha le mehal (the church calls this language tongues). His body appears lifeless, no movement, eyes open and blood oozing from his head – I've never stared into someone's eyes so deeply, there is where I made a connection with his soul – all of my love poured from my eyes to his eyes.

The people crowded around, they PROTESTESTED, "OH, HE GONE." "HE DID." Sister moving everyone away from him and I. "Hang in there," I said as I continued to look into his eyes, "I'm here, only listen to my voice, I'm here, I love you hold on fight, come on fight." And for the first time he moves his hands like a baby waving goodbye, "That's right, fight." And then I hear the sirens, they're here - it's ok, they're here. Sirens come and everyone disappears but not me, I want to ride with him to the hospital to make sure they take care of him, to make sure he knows.

Everyone leaves the scene and I discover why – they take him away and there we are taped off inside the crime scene forbidden to leave, treated like criminals in questioning.

"I'm not a criminal and I will not have a seat on the ground."

CRIME SCENE

"Ma'amm so what exactly did you see?"

"I didn't see anything, I heard the gunshots but just his body lay there alone"

"You say you seen the guy run off?"

"No that's not what I said"

"why are you putting words in my mouth?"

"Ma'am I need you to sit on the ground"

"I'm not a criminal and I will not have a seat on the ground"

"Well, you're going to have to ride to the station for questioning"

People standing around police with their pens and pads and all I can think about is the stop snitching DVDs from back in the day.

"No I will not ride in your car, down to the station with everyone watching thinking I'm telling a story about what I did not see"

"Well you said you saw"

"I told you what I saw and I came out to be by his side until help arrived – I didn't want him to be alone."

"Why is it that you're treating us like criminals?"

Black bodies, Lifeless in the city streets

Oh but there's someone praying

God still has dreams for me and he's in control of everything

SURE OF MYSELF,
JUST ENOUGH

I've gotten my posture back
You know head up high, shoulders wide – back straight
sure of herself girl
Sure, just enough for the weight of the world's views to
slide down and roll right off of me
I've gotten my posture back after I've lived a little
And the world tried to make me see through its eyes
When God had already given me blinders to see with
his eyes and it's no surprise to me that I've gotten my
posture back.
Sure of myself girl, sure that no matter what it seems
God still has dreams for me and he's in control of everything
So, I hold my head up high, square my shoulders, keep
my back straightened
I've gotten my posture back
Sure of myself – just enough to see on the level that was
created for me

How do you see yourself?

IT HURTS NOW, BUT LATER

It hurts now, but later
Later you won't feel a thing
Later will be now and you'll look back and smile
And you'll be happy you made it
You'll be happy you saved it
You saved a little bit of love in your heart for now
The now that came later
It hurts now, but later.....

Remember how you got here
Blood sweat and tears – prayers and fears.
Leaping, falling, stumbling, crawling
Bruises to the soul
Oh, oh, oh but you – you kept going
Remember how you got here
You kept going.

The only way to win is to never give up,
keep going.
Listen to that tiny voice within.
It's whispering to you – keep going.

How can you be glad
when it looks like
death all around you?

At first freedom couldn't read, all
it could do was dream
Dream of a better day when
whips didn't come the way of
the back and masters slap didn't
touch her face
And anger couldn't find her in
the cotton gens
When love was a thing worth
imagining
But still they had it
My ancestors still loved
That's when love wasn't such a
commodity
because it was being taken
in robbery
Your wife may get sold away to
another man's home
And all you had was dreams
And love to take care of you
No amount of money could buy
back your heart as it was sold on
the auction block
Yet they never knew it wasn't
for sale and hell, *no amount of hell
could make you lose hope then*
as you smiled on the inside as the
whips pierced your outside

Hoping for a better day
hoping, praying to a God
Oh God was important then
They taught him to you
Not knowing that once you had
an idea you would pray
Pray for freedom
Hope, Hope for a future for
your kids
And that which you prayed for
God would remember
And he'd tell you – that they
would see it
Freedom – one day
*This day, this is the day, this is the
day that the lord has made, let us
rejoice, let us rejoice and be glad in it*
But how?
*How can you be glad when it looks
like death all around you?*
Faith in that which you can't see
redirect your vision to the
place within
it's where hope lives
Just a little bit of hope shall carry
you through

FREE(ER)
THAN BEFORE

They marching, they rallying
They petitioning your kids
They free – free(er) than before
Your prayers are answered
They marching, they rallying
They petitioning
They boycotting your kids
They free – free(er) than before
But they want more
Your prayers have been answered?

What do you need to release to move forward / be free?

—

UNDEFILED

—

This is she before mommy had to return to the house for only God knows what. Maybe so I could have this story, share this story, heal from this story possibly free another young lady's mind from thoughts of Mr. Lacies hand between her not yet thighs because she's too young and meat on her bones does not exist. Her shorts fight to stay on her waist because she's so thin that momma has to use a safety pin.

But his hands are allowed to be there and this is the place it begins. "Sit on my lap young lady, baby girl, sweetheart, wife, woman, sexy, damn girl you fine." "Have a seat on my lap." "Ok." She 6, not 26, not 16 but 6 and he no,not 6, not 26, not 36 but closer to 56 and he has an eye for momma's baby –maybe momma wasn't enough — I guess she, she was the appetizer before the meal. His amuse Bouche Petite little thing she was maybe because momma couldn't afford to nourish her properly with anything accept her favorites,twisty doughnuts, oodles of noodles (tap ramen) to those new to it. But this is back when stoops were still white because grandmas cleaned them with soap and water and a little bit of bleach on their hands and knees scrubbing "WE FREE" put it like this, this was back before police cameras were in Baltimore – Maybe? ...No it wouldn't have saved she.

NO
TRESPASSING

~~UNDER~~ ~~24 HOUR~~
~~VIDEO~~ ~~SURVEILLANCE~~

TRESPASSERS WILL
BE PROSECUTED

They marching, They rallying
They petitioning your kids
They free
Free(er) than before?

Free your mind. What happened to you does not have to define you. Live with love in your heart – pursue that which is good in all areas of your life. Live with the peace of that which is true – that The God of the universe has good intentions for you. Believe, believe, believe and remove the shackles from your mind – this is the only way to escape this slavery, it is within.

They marching
They rallying
They petitioning your kids

It knew my name GRATEFUL.

GRATEFUL

Grateful for the hmmmm in my spirit and
the song in my heart
It's a hopeful, joyous sound – thank God
Grateful for that compliment she gave
My beauty startled her
"Oh, how beautiful you are," she says, when
she sees me for the first time.
Grateful for the movement of my lips
I can say so much and yet I say just enough
Grateful for the time when just enough was
too much
And I said it anyway
Grateful that courage still accompanies love
And the both of them still love me
Grateful that before I knew of love
It knew my name
GRATEFUL.

What are you grateful for? (simplicity is power).

——

he holds my heart and caresses my strings

LOVE SONG

His love is like music which he so elegantly plays
He holds my heart and caresses my strings
The violin of my heart plays the sweetest song in which he sings
The music from every note
Travels my soul
It's always on key
For it is his song that he plays for me

We laughed and I lay my head on his shoulder as he sang.

BACK WHEN
SUNDAY'S SANG

Sundays at the dinner table were my favorite time of the week,
I had just witnessed him preach/teach and stir up the presence
of the Holy Spirit and here we were at the dinner table having
waited for this moment all week.
Family time at the table I listened to him philosophize, post
sermon preach. We laughed and I lay my head on his shoulder as
he sang.

Such a beautiful song were those times

BEAUTIFUL DAY

My subconscious mind loves to dream
of the time that I spent with you
But then I awake to just the scent
of you on my sheets
Beneath the smells essence
are the thoughts of your presence
It is truly a blessing
to experience a love so intense
Is this my reality, or your immortality?
That you bring to my mortal being
That has me seeing stars early in the am
This is a beautiful day
My mind is still feigning, well dreaming of you
When I thought I was awake
I realize it was my unconscious mind
consciously thinking of you
And with eyes closed
Before I rose the sun's rays lit up my eyelids
But before I could invite it in,
the invitation had been sent
Then there was no choice
but to welcome it
Upon my face and with the sweetest embrace
The suns subtle temperature gives peace to my soul
I could stay here forever in this moment
Then the breeze through my window
interrupts my thoughts
And whistles through my linen nighty
This triggers the thought of you
And with a slight arousal
I think to myself this is going to be a beautiful day
Overwhelmed I feel an emotion,
it shoots through my body
With eyes open again for the first time
Everything appears new, yet familiar
No longer anonymous
Revealed is the feeling of love
Life in the form of a love story
As my foot touches the floor

A place that's just outside of heavens doorway

The feeling of the first step says
thank you for your touch
And with the second step
that rose me from the bed
Your welcome is said
Without a single word being spoken
The energy of love is flowing
Throughout my body
And spread onto my sanctuary
Which is wherever I go
Could I have traveled to a place
that's just outside of heaven's doorway?
Or is this
A beautiful day?

Kissing you, connects me to your soul

MAJESTIC CONNECTION

I love sharing in your energy
Your subtle intensity comforts me
Until you arrived I didn't know that something was missing
Kissing you, connects me to your soul
How old are you?
How old am I?
Here on earth in this human form
But my spirit has connected with yours
And I question my very own existence
Am I some majestic being?
That has reunited with her very reason for being?
Oh how I love sharing in your energy
Your subtle intensity comforts me
hey, I know this feeling – it's where I've belonged all along.

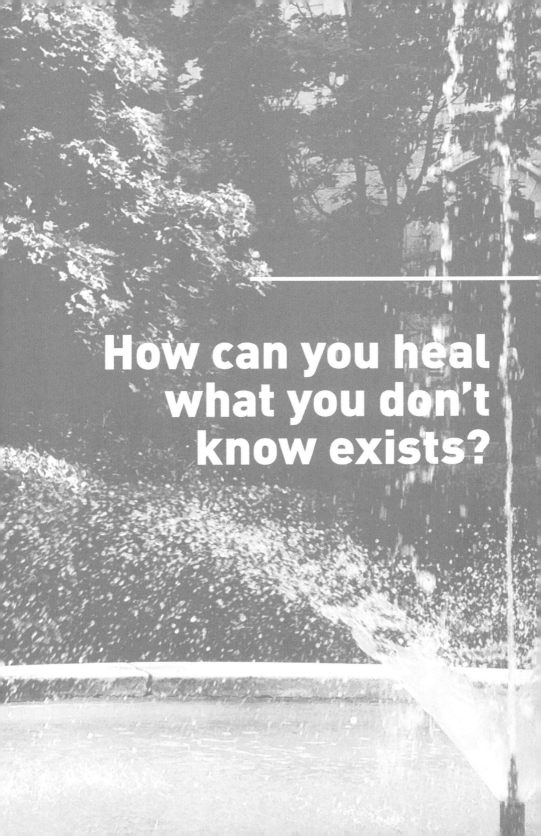

How can you heal
what you don't
know exists?

LOVE HER

If I could have loved her differently I would have
But then I had no idea of what she needed
I didn't know that she was insecure
I had never seen her confident before
How can you heal what you don't know exists?
If I could've loved her differently I would have
I didn't know that she was afraid
She always appeared to be so brave
She fought for all those around her
I never realized she didn't fight for me
I watched her in awe
thinking how strong she appeared to be
She carries the weight of everyone she knows
And you wouldn't know if she was tired
Because she carries it with a smile
If I could have loved her differently - I would have
I would have told her it's ok to put the baggage down
and rest awhile
I would have told her, "rest a while longer."

Putting it down makes you stronger
I would have told her there is joy in the
morning time
after you've rested a while
If I would've known I would have loved her
differently
I would have hugged her more
And told her she was created beautifully
I would have spent more time with her alone
Alone looking at her bare face, staring her in
her eyes
I would have asked her if she needed anything
"Is everything ok?"
And she would have declined my help
And I would have insisted
I would have loved her differently
had I known to love her was to love me
If I would have known
And now that I know – I shall love her differently.

What will you do to love yourself better / different than before?

—

YOU

There was a moment with you where I felt as
if I were standing in the middle of the universe
on a cloud. I had become one with you as the
stars shined in the morning time and your breath
breathed on mine and I inhaled every bit of you. I
felt you as the record played and I don't remember
the song just the feeling – I wouldn't even have
known there was music except I danced with you.
You're the music, treble, bass, rhythm and blues.
You and I are peaceful moments, we are on a cloud
in the middle of the universe and we - we are the
song. *We are the record that plays for the stars*; we are
what the universe delights in. I marvel at it and it
marvels at us.

I speak of peace and love

INFINITY

I have to leave you here
I would say Sorry to leave but I won't
Because that would imply that I don't want
to go and I do
This journey is about ME -how selfish?
It's about me being a blessing
To the many souls on this path of eternity
A never ending path of light
I must keep traveling
So the light can become brighter
The light now lives on my tongue
I speak of peace and love
I am guided to the light
And I am that which I press towards
I am that I am and that I am is truth
It's free and it is freed
The spirit dwelleth in me
I am gratitude with skin
I am empathy coated with strength
I wear it; I wear it in a place that you can't
see with your eyes
But I do wear it and you sense it
You feel its connection
And it wakes up apart of you
And it hugs you
you feel safe

You feel protected – it is love
I had to leave that old place
It was good for that space
But I'm increasing the space within
And I'm writing this world on the outside
So that you may see the light
Feel the light
Not selfish at all - I'm sharing the light
You now stand in a sacred place
Standing in the midst of holiness
It's all within me
I had to leave that part of me
I shed its skin
I had to go – I won't say sorry
That would imply that the divine plan isn't
worthy
That would suggest that the divine is
separate from me
That would resist what is destiny
And it is my only desire to stay on this true
and divine path of light
Love have your way
Love guide the way
Thank You Love

Nora is Words

I grew up in Baltimore City and have had the privilege of experiencing many different environments that have shaped the human being that I am today. Baltimore has made me empathetic to the suffering that many endure who are nameless to the world but not in the eyes of God. It has inspired me to write the stories of those who will never have the chance to tell their story. Baltimore has been a great teacher for me, a place that represented so much darkness from early childhood memories, but showed that out of the darkness can emerge a powerful, and strong being of light and love. I know that my being born in Baltimore City, during the time that I was born to the family that I was born is no mistake it was purposed. Purpose yet to be fully revealed but this book is dedicated to Baltimore City.

Thank You

I would like to say thank you to the pain that I have endured – because of the pressure you applied, I have gained a supernatural strength. Thank you to the darkness that I have had to maneuver through because of you, my insight (inward sight) has deepened and my appreciation for self is unprecedented.

Thank you to my book designer Brubey Hu — a kind spirit and an excellent creative

Thank you to Mateo Blu who did my cover design, a passionate soul expressionist artist

Thank you to all my friends and family who have loved me on my journey in life and through the process of the completion of this book. It is truly an honor to be a person who can express life, my life, and others through words.

Words have healed me — thank you for the words that always find their way through the ink.

CONTENTS

Made in the USA
Middletown, DE
19 April 2023

28896482R00077